To

From

Published by Candle Books
an imprint of
Lion Hudson plc
Wilkinson House, Jordan Hill Road,
Oxford OX2 8DR, England
www.lionhudson.com/candle

ISBN 978 1 78128 176 5
e-ISBN 978 1 78128 204 5

First edition 2015

A catalogue record for this book is available from the British Library

Printed and bound in Singapore, February 2015, LH01

My Little Picture Bible

By Juliet David
Illustrated by Elina Ellis

CANDLE BOOKS

Contents

The beginning

In the beginning, God made heaven and earth.
Everything was completely dark.
So God said, "Let there be light!"
And there was light.
God saw it was good.
And that was day one!

Next...

On day two, God put water in the sea
and clouds in the sky.
On day three he made dry land, seas, and rivers.
God said, "Let the earth be green!"
Grasses, trees, and flowers sprang up.
And God saw that it was *all* good.

Sun and stars

On day four God put the sun in the sky
to warm the earth.
The night was very dark,
so God put the moon and the stars in the sky.
Then he made spring, summer, autumn, and winter.
It was *all* good.

Fish in the sea

On day five God made all sea creatures:
sharks and turtles; shellfish and crabs.
And God made all the birds and
insects: eagles and sparrows;
wasps, flies, and bees.
Every shape and size of flying thing.
God saw that it was *all* good.

All God's creatures

On day six God said,
"Let there be living things on land!"
So he created dogs, horses, and camels;
lions, lizards, and snails;
worms, wombats, and warthogs.

And God saw it was good.
Everything was good.
But there were no people!

Adam and Eve

So God said, "I shall create humans."
God made the first man, Adam.
And the first woman, Eve.

"Now start a family!"
God told them.
"Let your family spread
across the whole earth."

The first garden

God gave Adam and Eve a beautiful garden to live in. The Garden of Eden.

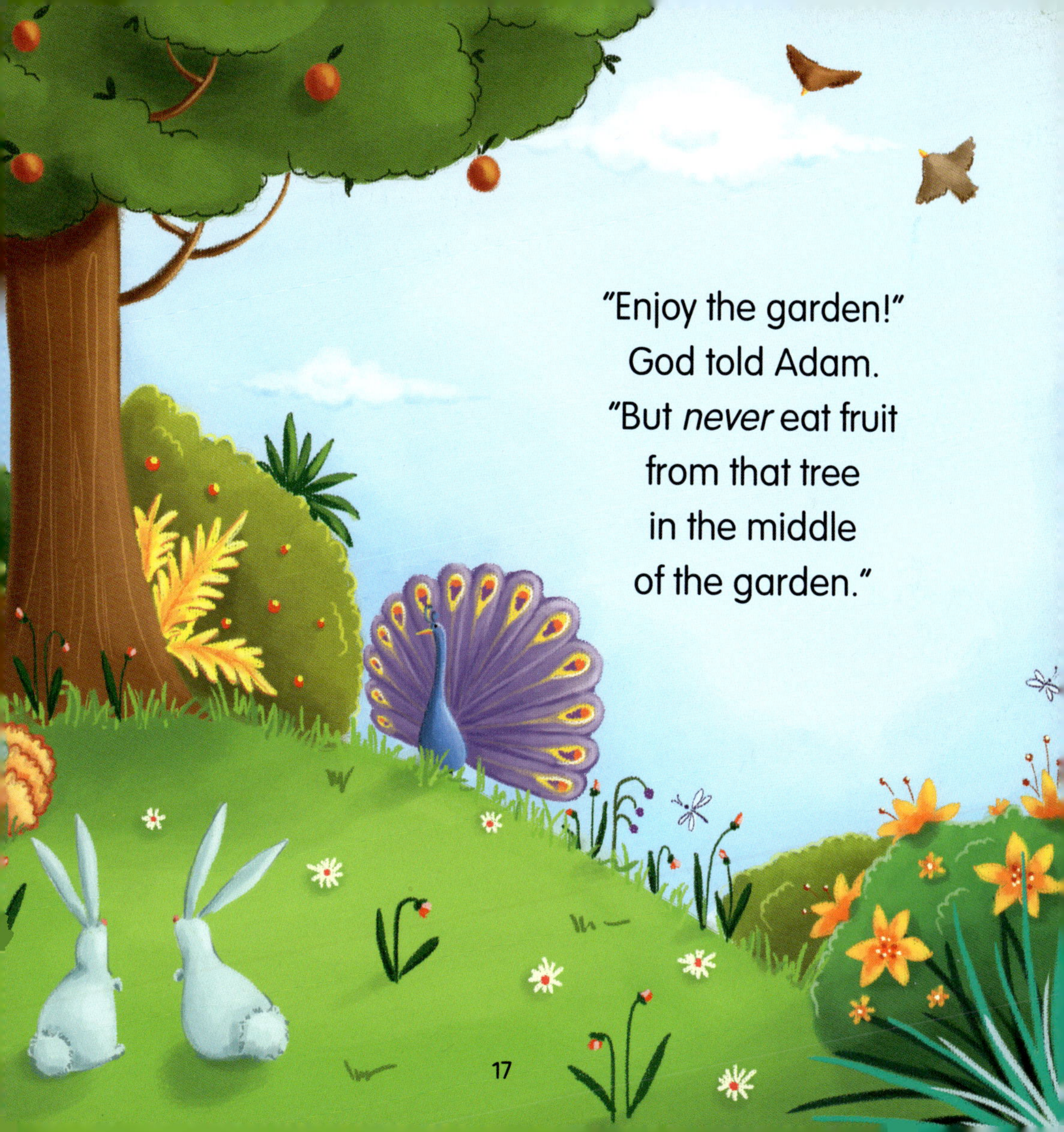

"Enjoy the garden!"
God told Adam.
"But *never* eat fruit
from that tree
in the middle
of the garden."

Forbidden

One day a snake slithered up to Eve.
"Take a bite of *that* fruit," he hissed.
"But we mustn't eat that!"
said Eve.
"Just one *tiny* bite!"
said the snake.

So Eve took a bite.
Adam came to find her,
Eve said,
"Here, taste this
delicious fruit!"
And Adam took a bite too.

Leaving the garden

That evening God came to the garden.
"Where are you?" God called to them.
"Why are you hiding?"
"Eve gave me the fruit – so I ate it,"
said Adam.

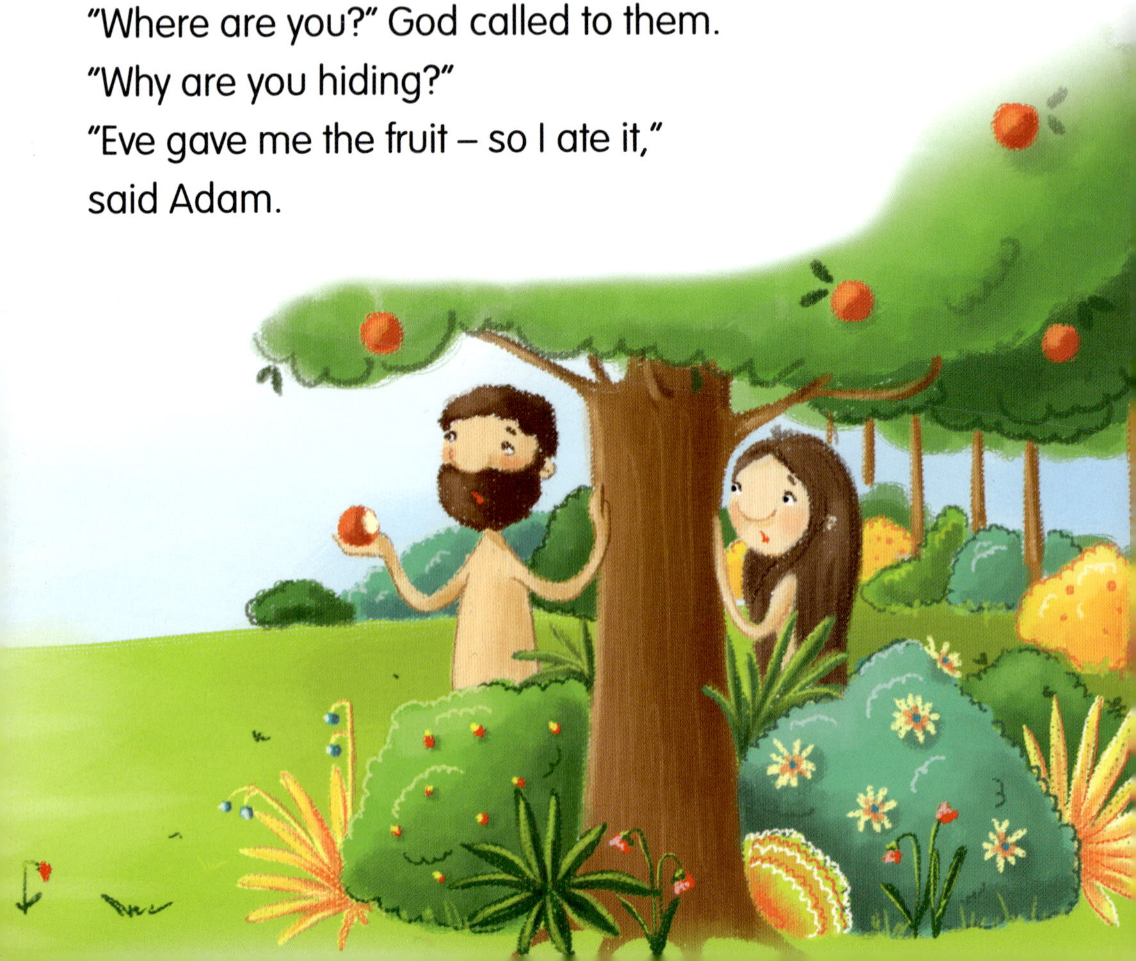

"The snake tricked me," said Eve.
Adam and Eve had disobeyed God.
So he sent them out of the garden forever.
Now they had to work hard, digging and sowing.
They often thought of the happy times in Eden.

Noah builds an ark

Years later, many people were living on earth.
Just one man, Noah, was good.
"A great flood is coming,"
said God.
"Build a huge boat, Noah.
Then fill it with your family
and two of *every* sort of animal."
Noah did just that.
He built a huge boat
– Noah's ark.
Then he filled it
with his family
and two of *every* sort of animal.

The last animal climbed on board.
Then the rain started.
It rained so hard, water soon covered the hills.
But the ark floated on the water.
Noah, his family, and all the animals were safe inside.
God helped Noah escape from the flood.

After forty days and nights,
the rain stopped.
But there was still water everywhere.
One day Noah sent out a dove.
The dove flew back,
carrying a green leaf in its beak.
Hooray! Plants were growing again!
It was time to come out of the ark.
Noah, his family, and all
the animals left the boat.
Afterwards, God put a
beautiful rainbow in
the sky.
"I will *never* flood the
whole earth again,"
he promised.

The tallest tower

At this time everyone spoke the same language.
Some men started to build a really tall tower.
"We'll reach right up to heaven!" they boasted.
God was angry when he heard this.
So he made everyone
speak a different language.
Nobody could understand
what anybody else
was saying!
So the tall tower
never got finished.

Abraham leaves home

In a land called Ur lived a man named Abraham.
He was married to Sarah.
"Leave your home!" said God.
"I'm going to give you
a special new land!"
Abraham and Sarah
believed God.
So they set out
to find this new land –
the Promised Land.

After a very long journey,
they arrived in their new land.
Here they could graze their sheep
and feed their cattle.

A baby for Sarah

Abraham and Sarah were very old.
But they badly wanted a baby.
One day God sent three visitors
to Abraham.
"Sarah *will* have a
baby," they said.

Sarah just laughed!
She didn't believe them.
But soon Sarah had a baby boy
– just as God promised.
Abraham and Sarah
called their
son Isaac.

A wife for Isaac

Isaac grew up. He wanted to find himself a wife.
So Abraham sent his servant to find a wife for Isaac.
The servant journeyed many days.
"If a woman gives water for your camels," God told him,
"*she* will be Isaac's wife!"

One evening a beautiful woman came to the well.
"Would you like water for your camels?" she asked.
So Abraham's servant knew she should be Isaac's wife.
Her name was Rebekah.

Twins!

Isaac and Rebekah soon married
– and Rebekah had twin sons.
The older boy was red and hairy: he was named Esau.
The younger twin was named Jacob.

One day Esau was very hungry.
"Let me have some soup!"
he asked Jacob.
"Give me your rights
as Isaac's oldest son,"
said Jacob.
"*Then* you can have
some soup."
Esau stupidly agreed.

Jacob's dream

Later Esau realized Jacob had tricked him.
He was furious!
Jacob was so scared of his brother that he ran away.
One night Jacob was sleeping in the desert.
He had a wonderful dream.
He saw stairs to heaven.
Angels were walking up and down.
"I will look after your family," God promised Jacob.

Joseph the dreamer

Jacob had twelve sons.
But he loved Joseph more than all the rest.
One day Jacob gave Joseph a beautiful coat.
This made his brothers *really* jealous.

Sometimes Joseph had dreams.
"I dreamt we all had bundles of grain," he told his brothers.
"Then your bundles bowed down to mine."
"So you think we will bow down to you?"
they asked him angrily.

One day Joseph's brothers were working far from home.
He took them some food.
"Let's sell Joseph
to those traders,"
said his cruel brothers.
These traders
took Joseph away
to the land
of Egypt.

Things soon got even worse for Joseph.
He had to work very hard for a man in Egypt.
But this man's wife told lies about Joseph.
"He tried to attack me!" she said.
So they threw poor Joseph into jail.
But God had a plan for him.

One night the king of Egypt had strange dreams.
His wise men had no idea what his dreams meant.
Suddenly one of the king's servants said,
"I was in prison – and Joseph explained my dream."
"Send for Joseph immediately!"
ordered Pharaoh.

They brought Joseph from jail to the king.
"In my dream there were seven fat cows," said the king.
"Seven thin cows came and swallowed them!"
"This means for seven years there will be good harvests," said Joseph. "But then there will be seven years with no rain – and no harvest."

"Fill up my barns with grain," the king told Joseph.
"Then we can feed the people in the hungry years.
Now Joseph brought his family to live in Egypt.
They became known as the "Israelites".

Moses saves his people

Many years after Joseph died, a wicked king said,
"Throw *every* Israelite baby boy into the river."
One Israelite mother hid her baby in a basket
and floated it in the river.

The princess of Egypt came to the river to bathe.
She saw the baby in the basket. She loved the little boy.
She called him Moses, and took him to her palace to live.
God kept baby Moses safe.

Moses grew up in the king's palace.
But later he became a shepherd in the desert.
One day he noticed something very strange.
A bush in the desert was on fire
– but it just kept burning!
Suddenly God spoke to him from the flames.
"Go back to Egypt," God said.
"The king of Egypt is making Israelites work as slaves.
Tell the king of Egypt to let my people go!"

Moses went to the king's
palace, as God told him.
"God says,
'Let my people go!'"
he told the king.
"But I don't *know*
your God,"
said the king.
"Why should
I obey him?"
Instead the king
made the Israelites
work even harder.
Then terrible things
started to happen to
the Egyptians.

Each time something bad happened,
the king said the Israelites could leave.
Afterwards, he changed his mind.
One terrible night,
the oldest boy in every
Egyptian family died.
Then at last the king
said to Moses,
"*Go!* Leave Egypt!
Take your people
and *go*."
God's people
were free at last!

The Israelites left Egypt and marched into the desert.
But soon the king of Egypt changed his mind again.

He sent his army to chase after the Israelites.
They had reached the shores of the Red Sea.
But there was no way to get across it!

"Hold up your stick!" God told Moses.
He did – and the water parted.
Moses led his people on a dry path across the sea.

Rules for living

The Israelites trudged on through the hot desert.
Moses climbed a rocky mountain to meet God.
"I'm going to give you my rules for living,"
God told him.
"I will write them on two big,
flat stones."
We call these rules the
"Ten Commandments".

Crossing the river

The Israelites reached the River Jordan.
Across it was the land God promised them – Canaan.
The priests carried a golden box.
Inside were the Ten Commandments.
The priests walked into the water.

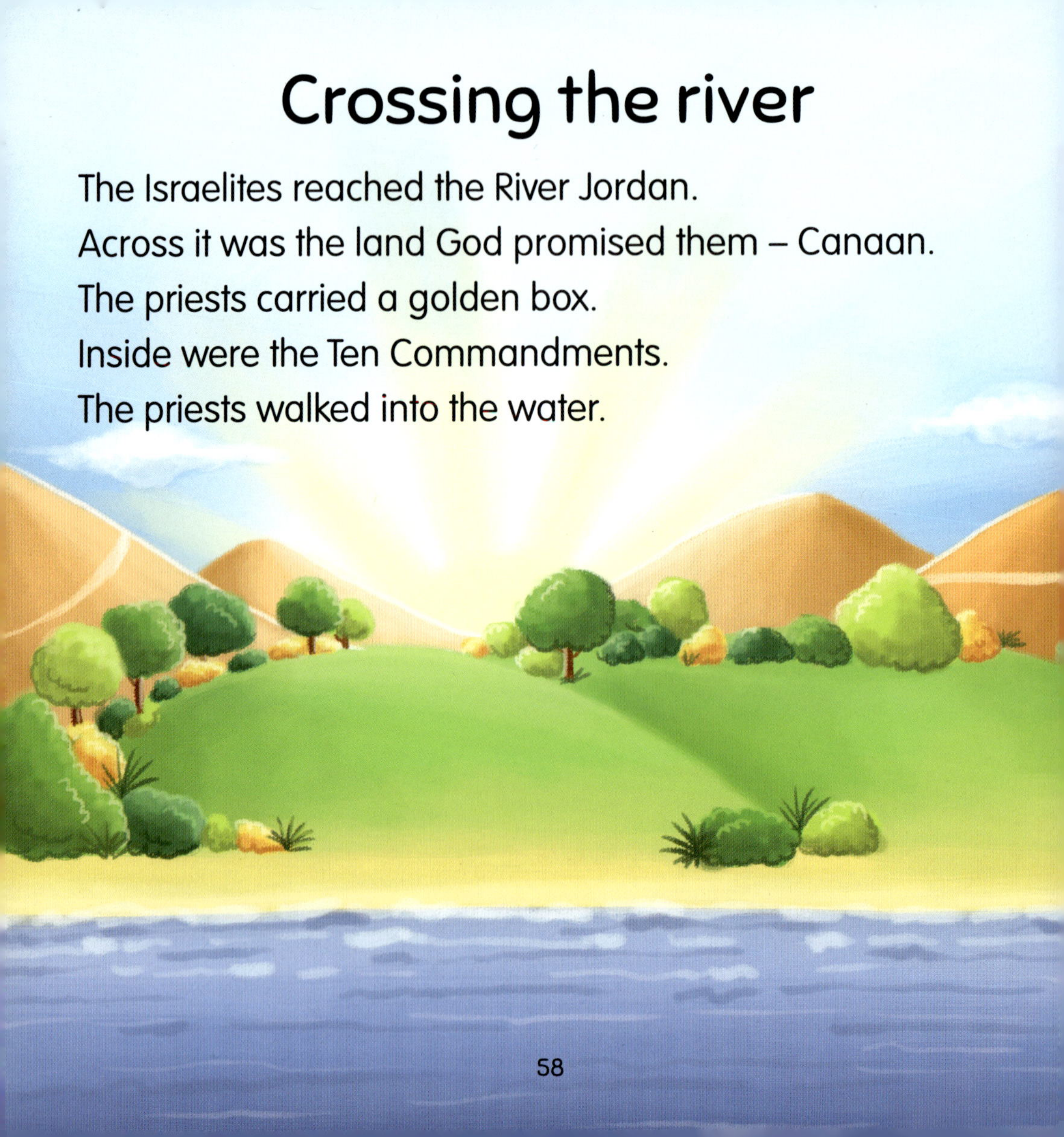

Immediately a dry path opened up!
The people followed the priests across the river.
When everyone was over the river, it flooded back.
The Israelites had arrived in the Promised Land!

A city collapses

Now God gave the Israelites a new leader, named Joshua.
Joshua took his army to the great city of Jericho.
"March around the walls of Jericho for six days," God said.
"On the seventh day, march around seven times.
Then blow your trumpets and shout as loud as you can!"
The Israelites did as God told them
– and the city collapsed.

A frightened soldier

One day an angel visited
a farmer named Gideon.
"God wants you to save
your people!" said the angel.
Gideon felt very scared.
But he gathered up an army.

Gideon gave each soldier a trumpet and a jar.
While the enemy was asleep, Gideon's men blew their trumpets, smashed their pots, and waved flames.
The enemy soldiers ran away terrified.

The man with long hair

"You're going to have a special son!" an angel told one Israelite woman. "But don't cut his hair. *Ever!*

"His long hair will show he has a special job to do for God."

The woman named her son Samson. He grew very strong. Then one day enemies cut off his hair. His strength vanished and they threw him in jail.

In prison, Samson's hair grew and his strength returned.

His enemies had a party. They took Samson along and made fun of him.

Samson pushed the pillars of the building – and it fell on his cruel enemies.

The kind farmer

Ruth lived with her mother-in-law, Naomi.
One day Ruth went to a farmer's fields to gather grain.
The farmer said, "Take all the grain you need."
He loved Ruth. They married and had a little boy.

Samuel listens to God

"Lord, give me a son," Hannah prayed.
"When he grows up, I'll give him to help in your temple."
Eli, the chief priest, was listening.
"Go home, Hannah!" said Eli. "God has heard you."
Sure enough, she soon had a son.
"We'll call our baby Samuel,"
she said.
"I'll give him to
help in the temple,
just as I promised."

When Samuel was old enough,
Hannah took him to help Eli the priest.
One night, Samuel heard a voice call, *"Samuel!"*
He thought it was Eli, and ran to the old man.
"Here I am, Eli!" he said. "You called me."

"I didn't call," said Eli. "Go back to bed."
The same thing happened three times.
Then Eli knew it must be God calling Samuel.
"If you hear the voice again," said Eli,
"Say, 'Speak, Lord – I am listening.'"
Soon the voice came again,
"Samuel! Samuel!"
He answered,
"Speak, Lord – I am listening!"
God told Samuel he would
become a leader of Israel.

A king for Israel

Samuel grew up and ruled the Israelites wisely.

One day some people came to him.

"We want a king to rule over us!" they said.

So Samuel tried to find them a king.

Saul was very, very tall.

"He looks *just* like a king!" thought Samuel.

"This is your king," he told the people.

"God save the king!" they shouted.

So Saul became the first king of Israel.

Another king

But Saul did things
that saddened God.
So God sent Samuel
to find a new king.
Samuel visited a man
who had many sons.
But none of them
seemed right to be king.
"Do you have any more
sons?" asked Samuel.
"There's young David,"
said the man.
"He's minding the sheep!"
"*He* will be the next king
of Israel," God told Samuel.

David beats a giant

A huge giant called Goliath was bullying God's people.
"I will fight this giant!" said David.
He had only his shepherd's sling.

David's stone hit the giant
and he fell to the ground.
God helped little David
beat the giant Goliath.

David runs away

David often played the harp for King Saul.
But people were saying, "David's braver than King Saul!"
So Saul grew jealous of David.
One day he threw
a spear at him.
David ran away
to the desert.
Saul hunted for him.
But God kept David safe.
One day King Saul
died in battle.
Now David was
crowned king –
just as Samuel
had promised.

The wisest king

After David died, his son Solomon became king.

"What gift would you like most?" God asked Solomon.
"Please, Lord, make me wise," replied King Solomon.
"I will make you wiser than *anyone* who ever lived," God promised.

One day two women brought a baby to King Solomon.
"It's *my* baby!" shouted one woman.
"No! It's *mine*!" yelled the other.
"Cut the baby in half!"
ordered Solomon.
"Give the women half each!"
"No! Don't do that!"
shrieked one woman.
"I'd rather *she* have the baby
than it was cut in two."
Wise King Solomon knew
this woman was the real mother.
She had a true mother's
love for her child.

A temple for God

King Solomon built a wonderful temple, where the Israelites could pray to God.

Priests carried the golden
box containing the
Ten Commandments
into the Temple.
The Temple filled
with dazzling light,
to show God was
with his
people.

A very bad king

Elijah, one of God's helpers,
ran away to the desert.
He could find nothing to eat.
"Lord, give me some food!" he prayed.
Soon, birds flew over, carrying meat in their beaks.
God looked after Elijah in the desert.

Lots of oil!

Elisha was another of God's helpers.
One day Elisha met a woman.
"I'm so hungry!" she said.
"I have only one tiny pot of oil."
"Borrow lots of jars," said Elisha.
"Then pour your oil into them."
She did – and the oil
just kept coming!
She filled every
jar in the house.
The woman took the jars of oil
to market and sold them.
Soon she had enough money to buy
plenty of food for her family.
God's prophet Elisha helped her.

A nasty disease

Naaman had a horrible skin disease called leprosy.
"Elisha's God could help you," his servant told him.
So Naaman set off to find Elisha.
"I have this nasty skin disease," explained Naaman.
"Go, wash in the river
seven times," said Elisha.
"Then you'll be well again!"
It sounded a bit silly.
But Naaman dipped
himself in the river.
After the seventh time,
the leprosy vanished!
His skin was clear again.
God healed him.

A brave queen

Esther was a Jewish girl who married the king of Persia. One day she heard a man called Haman making a plot. "I will kill all Queen Esther's people, the Jews," he said.

Esther invited Haman and the king to a banquet.
"Haman plans to kill my people," she said at dinner.
The king was very angry. He arrested Haman.
Esther was brave; she saved her people.

Saved from lions!

Daniel prayed to God three times *every* day.
One day the king ordered:
"Anyone who prays will be thrown to hungry lions."

"Daniel is still praying," sneaky men told the king.
So soldiers threw Daniel into a pit of roaring lions.
Daniel prayed, "Lord, save me!"
God sent an angel to shut those hungry lions' mouths.

Rescued!

"Go to the great
city of Nineveh,"
God told Jonah.
"Tell the people they
must stop doing
bad things."
But Jonah ran away!

He sailed off in a boat.
A fierce storm blew,
so the sailors flung
Jonah into the sea.
He thought he
was going to drown.
Then – *gulp!*
– something swallowed Jonah.

Jonah found himself inside the tummy of a great fish.
After three days the fish spat Jonah out on the shore.
God saved Jonah from drowning.
"Go to Nineveh!" said God again.
This time Jonah did what God told him.

The first Christmas

One day an angel appeared to a woman called Mary. Mary was astonished – and a bit scared.

"Don't be worried,"
said the angel.
"I have *great* news!
You are going to have a baby.
You must call him Jesus!
God is sending him
to save the world."
Mary felt very happy.
"I will do whatever
God wants!" she said.

Mary loved Joseph, the village carpenter.
Now they got married.
It was almost time for Mary's baby to be born.
But they had to go to Joseph's home town, Bethlehem.
It was a long, tiring journey.
"Where are we going to sleep?" asked Mary.

Joseph knocked on the door of the inn.
"I'm sorry," said the innkeeper. "We're quite full!"
He saw Mary's tired face. "There is a little stable,"
he added. "You're welcome to stay there!"

In that stable, Mary's baby was born.
She named him "Jesus", as the angel told her.
"I've made a bed for baby Jesus," said Joseph.

It was dark in the fields near Bethlehem.
Suddenly the skies lit up.
An angel appeared.
The shepherds felt scared.
"Don't be afraid,"
said the angel.
"I bring good news!"

"Your king has been born, in Bethlehem.
You'll find him lying in a manger!"
Then a crowd of angels filled the sky, singing.
The shepherds rushed off to Bethlehem.
They found the stable and knelt before baby Jesus.

Far away in the East lived some wise men.
Every night they studied the skies.
Suddenly one said,
"I've never seen that star before!"
"It's a sign," said another.
"A new king has been born!"
"Let's follow the star
and find this new king."
So the wise men set out
on a long journey,
following the star.
They came at last to Bethlehem,
where they found Jesus.
They brought him rich presents:
gold, and precious scents
called frankincense and myrrh.

Lost!

When Jesus was twelve, Mary said, "Let's all go to the great festival in Jerusalem." There, in the Temple, Jesus met teachers and priests. Afterwards they started the journey home. Suddenly Joseph and Mary realized they'd lost Jesus. They went back to Jerusalem.

There they found Jesus in the Temple,
talking to the teachers.
"Didn't you *know* I'd be here?"
Jesus asked Mary.
"I had to come to
my Father's house."

A fresh start

John was Jesus' cousin. He lived in the desert.
He had a special job to do.
"You do a lot of bad things," he used to tell people.
"Change your ways and start doing what's right."
Crowds came to hear him.
"Be baptized!" he said.
"Make a fresh start!"
People called him "John the Baptist" because he baptized people in the River Jordan.

John baptizes Jesus

One day Jesus came to John.

"Please baptize me!" Jesus asked John.

"I should be baptized by *you,*" said John.
"But it's what God wants!" Jesus replied.
So John dipped Jesus in the River Jordan.
Then a dove flew over Jesus' head.
"This is my Son," said a voice. "I'm *so* pleased with him."

Jesus' team

One day Jesus was standing by Lake Galilee.
People crowded around, listening to his stories.
Jesus climbed into a boat that belonged
to a man called Peter.
Then he talked to the people
from the boat.
When he had finished,
Jesus said to Peter,
"Go deeper and
let down your nets.
"We fished all night
and caught *nothing,"*
said Peter.
"But for you we
will let down our
nets again."

This time the nets were so full that they started to tear.
Peter and his friends were amazed to see so many fish.
"From now on you'll be fishing for *people*!" said Jesus.
Peter, his brother Andrew, and their two friends,
James and John, all followed Jesus.

Another day Jesus saw a taxman named Matthew working at his desk.
"Follow me!" he called.
Matthew got up and followed Jesus.
Jesus called other men too:
Philip,
Bartholomew,
Thomas the twin,
another James,
Thaddaeus,
Simon,
and Judas Iscariot.
Twelve altogether.
They were Jesus' team, the disciples.

Water becomes wine

A man invited Jesus to his wedding party.
It wasn't long before they'd drunk all the wine.
"Fill those six big wine jars with water!" said Jesus.

Instantly the water changed into wine.
"This is the best wine ever!" people said.

A blind man sees

Some people brought a blind man to Jesus.
"Please help our friend to see!" they begged.

Jesus placed his hands over the man's eyes.
His eyes opened. Now the blind man could see!

Thank you!

Jesus met ten men with a skin disease called leprosy.

"*Please* help us!" they called to him.

"You are healed," said Jesus.

As the men walked home, the disease disappeared.

One man came back.

"Thank you, Jesus," he said.

"Where are all the others?" asked Jesus.

"You are the only one who came back to thank God."

A sick girl

A man called Jairus came running to Jesus.
"My little girl is terribly ill," he said. "Please help!"

Jesus hurried home with him.
But by the time they arrived, Jairus's daughter had died.
Jesus took her hand.
"Little girl, wake up!" he said.
At once she opened her eyes.
"Give her something to eat!" Jesus said to her mother.
Jesus helped the little girl come back to life.

Man through the roof

Another time some men carried a sick friend to Jesus.

The house was full so they let him down from the roof.

"Stand up!" Jesus said to him.

At once the sick man stood up.

Everyone was astonished.

Jesus helped this man to walk.

A hungry crowd

Jesus was telling stories to huge crowds in the country.
By evening everyone felt hungry – but they had no food!
One boy had just five loaves and two fish.
He gave them all to Jesus.
Jesus broke up the food and his friends gave it out.
There was enough for everyone!
There were even twelve baskets full of leftovers.

A walk on the lake

Jesus' friends were sailing across the lake. "I will follow you," said Jesus. They were only halfway across when a rough storm rose. The men had to row hard to stop the boat from sinking.

Suddenly they saw what they thought was a ghost!
But it was Jesus, walking on the water.
"Don't be afraid!" he called.
He climbed into the boat.
At once the wind calmed down.

The lost son

Jesus told this great story.

There was once a farmer who had two sons.

The younger son left home, taking his share of his dad's money.

The boy journeyed to a far country.
He had lots of money so he had lots of fun.
When the money ran out, he started looking after pigs.
One day he thought,
"I'd be better off as a servant in
my dad's house."
So he set off home.
When he arrived, his dad
gave a great party.
He said, "My son, who
was lost, is found!"
"God also welcomes
people who are
lost," Jesus added.

The helpful stranger

Jesus told this story too.

A man was on a journey when thieves beat him and robbed him.

A priest came along – but passed quickly by.

A man from the Temple came up – and walked past too.
Finally a stranger came down the road.
He stopped, cleaned the man's wounds,
and took him to an inn to get better.
"Which of these men was a true friend?" Jesus asked.
"The stranger!" said his listener.

Lost sheep

Jesus told this story too.
A shepherd once had 100 sheep.
One night he lost one of them, so he went to look for it.
At last he found his missing sheep.
He picked it up gently and carried it home.
"I'm so happy!" he said. "I found my lost sheep."

"God is like this good shepherd," said Jesus.
"He's glad when *anyone* comes to him."

Jesus and the children

One day some mothers brought their children to Jesus. "Jesus is *so* tired," said Jesus' friends. "Don't bother him!"

But Jesus heard what they were saying.

"Let the little children come to me!" he said. "Don't stop them! You must love God like a little child if you want to enter heaven."

The storm

Jesus was sailing across the lake with his friends.
He was tired and fell fast asleep.
Suddenly a storm arose.
The disciples were scared.
"*Jesus, wake up!*" they cried.
"We're all going to drown."
Jesus stood up.
"Storm – be quiet!" he said.
"Wind – stop!"
Everything was
calm again.

A tiny man

Zacchaeus was a tax collector.
He took more money than he should.
People hated him.
One day Zacchaeus heard Jesus was visiting town.
He was very short, so he climbed a tree to see Jesus.

Jesus stopped under that tree.
"Come down!" Jesus called. "I want to visit you."
After meeting Jesus, Zacchaeus was a better person.
He gave half his money to the poor.

The first Easter

Jesus was going to Jerusalem with his friends for the festival of Passover.

“I will be arrested and killed,” he told them.
“But after three days, I will be raised from the dead.”
His friends had no idea what he meant.

Jesus borrowed a donkey and rode into Jerusalem.
The crowds got very excited.
People spread their cloaks on the ground before Jesus.
Others waved branches from palm trees.
Soon everyone was shouting,
"*Hosanna!* Hooray for God!"

But priests from the Temple were plotting to kill Jesus.
"Pay me well!" said Judas, one of Jesus' friends.
"And I'll show you where you can arrest Jesus."
So the priests gave Judas thirty silver coins.

When Jesus reached Jerusalem,
he went straight to the Temple.
Lots of shopkeepers had set up tables there.

Jesus was very angry.
He threw over their tables.
"You're making God's Temple into a robbers' den!"
he shouted.

It was the night of the feast.
Jesus had supper with his twelve disciples.
"Love one another, as I love you," he said.
Jesus took some bread.

He thanked God for it and broke it.
He shared it with his friends.
Then Jesus took a cup of wine, and thanked God for it.
He passed it to his disciples.

After supper, Jesus took his friends to a garden.
"I want to pray alone," he said. "Please stay here and pray!"
Jesus came back and found them all asleep!
"*Wake up!*" he said. "Here come my enemies!"
Judas was coming with men carrying swords and sticks.

Judas walked up to Jesus and kissed him.
Then soldiers took Jesus prisoner.
His disciples ran off.

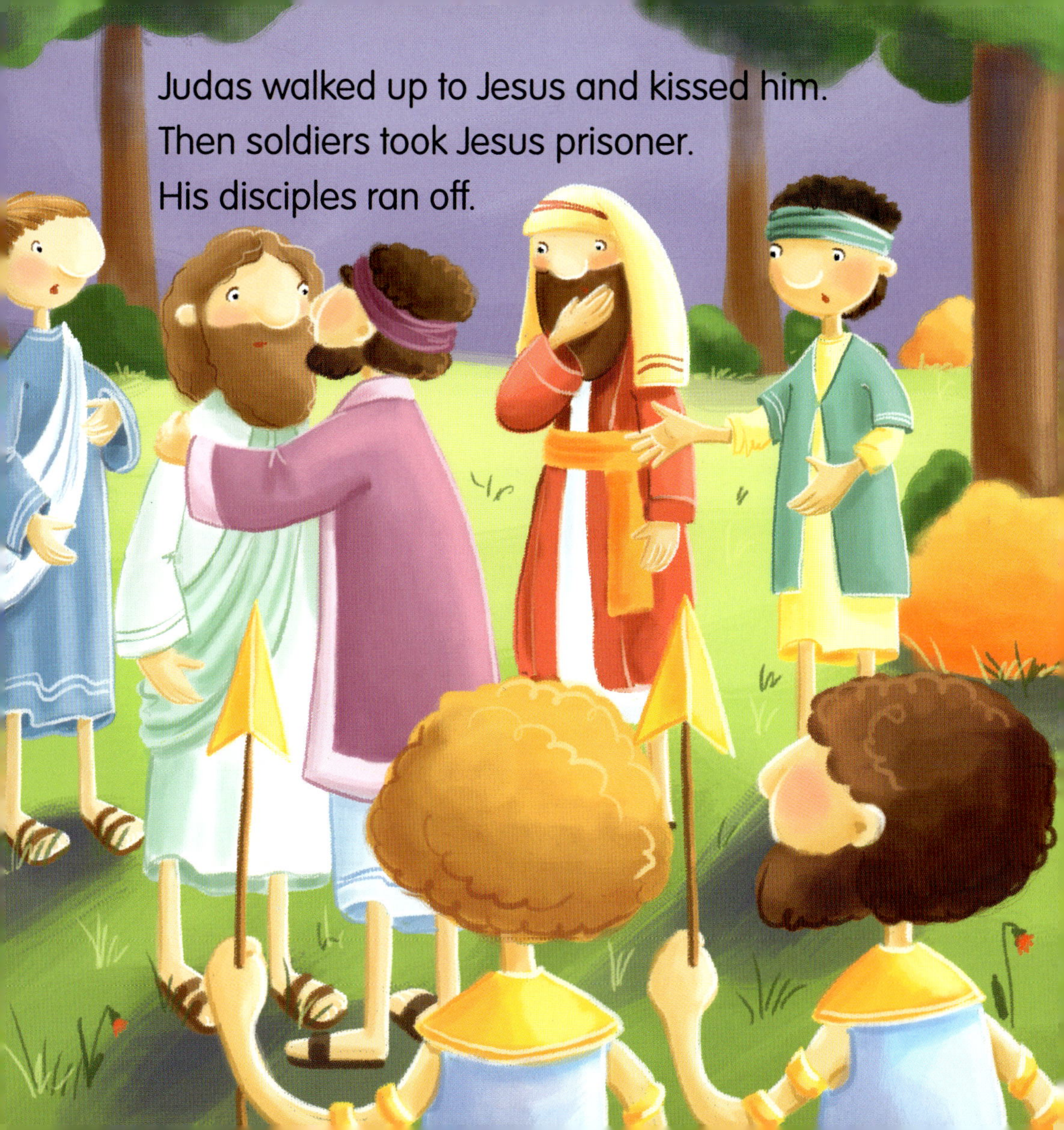

Next morning priests took Jesus to the ruler, Pilate.
"Jesus is making trouble," they said. "Put him to death!"
"I can find *nothing* wrong with him," said Pilate.
But the crowd shouted,
"Put him on a cross!"

"I will send him to die," said Pilate.

Roman soldiers marched Jesus to a hill near the city.
There they put him on a wooden cross.
They also put two robbers on crosses,
one each side of Jesus.

At midday, the sky went dark.
Three hours later, Jesus died.
Jesus' family and his friends stood watching sadly.

After Jesus died, a friend laid his body in a rock tomb.
He rolled a huge stone across the doorway.
Early Sunday morning,
Jesus' friend Mary visited the tomb.
She saw the big stone had been rolled away.
But she couldn't see Jesus' body.
She stood outside the tomb, crying.

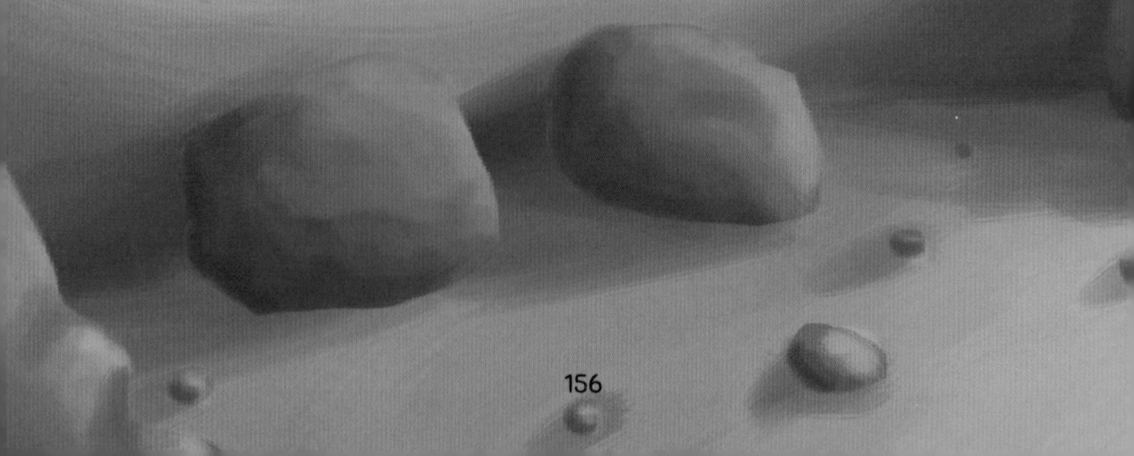

Mary looked round and saw a man
– she didn't realise it was Jesus.
He said, "Mary!"
Then she *knew* it was Jesus.
Mary rushed off to tell
the disciples,
"*Jesus is alive!*"

Later Jesus' disciples were
in a house together.
Suddenly Jesus appeared.
At first they were scared.
"Don't be afraid," said Jesus.
"God has brought me
back to life."

After this Jesus walked up a hill with his disciples.
"Now I am going to be with God," he said.
"But I am still with you. I always will be."
A cloud took Jesus away.
Then an angel appeared.
"Jesus is now with God in heaven," he said.
"One day he will return."